OLDHAM COLISEUM
—— THEATRE
The first hundred years

James Carter

Published in 1986
by Oldham Leisure Services
in association with the
Oldham Coliseum Theatre.

©James Carter 1986

Design: Keith Warrender

Printed by The Commercial
Centre Ltd., Hollinwood,
Oldham.

ISBN 0 902809 15 6

Acknowledgments
BBC Hulton Picture Library
John Lunn
Duncan Gurr
Derek Marshall
Cartoons on pp. 38 & 42 by
Jack Kirkbride
The late Kenneth Hirst and
Philip Hirst of the Oldham
Evening Chronicle.

*And thanks to all those people
whose support and
encouragement have kept the
Coliseum alive over the last
hundred years.*

Russell Dixon and Cliff Howells in 'Bent', 1980.

Sheila Price and Jean Alexander in 'Arsenic and Old Lace', 1974.

The cast of 'Girlfriends', 1986.

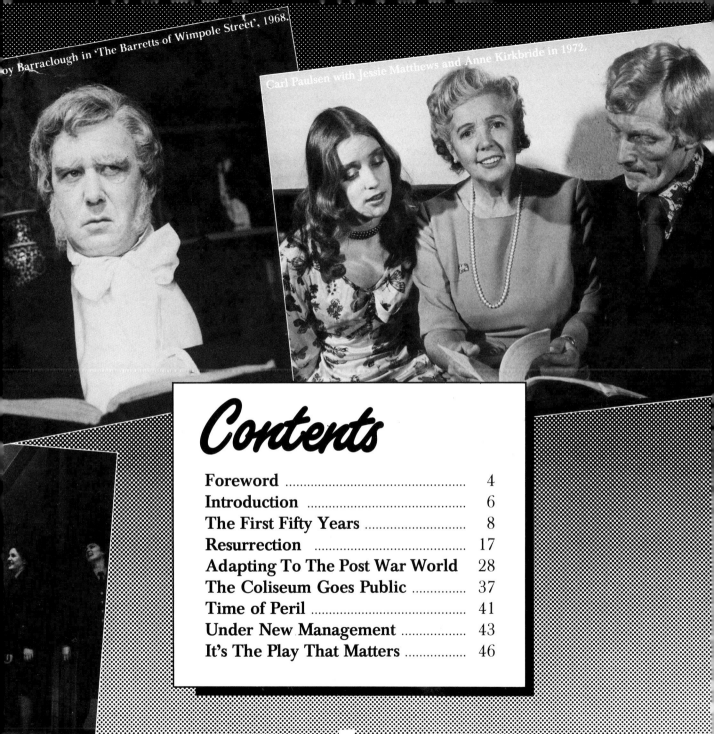

oy Barraclough in 'The Barretts of Wimpole Street', 1968.

Carl Paulsen with Jessie Matthews and Anne Kirkbride in 1972.

Contents

Foreword

"Entertain us, or be gone", wrote George Rowell towards the back end of the nineteenth century, and when all the trendy talking is over it boils down to just that.

Reading through Jim Carter's carefully compiled and scholarly history I am struck by the similarity of the problems of the past years, past board members, past chairmen. It is so true that nothing ever really changes.

I do hope that when some, as yet unborn, chronicler licks his 'blacklead' prior to starting on the history of "The Second Hundred Years" of this living, salty, stimulating and sometimes infuriating place, he will at least grant that we did our best.

RAY WHITEHEAD
Chairman, Oldham Coliseum Theatre Ltd.

"If it had not been for the Oldham Coliseum Theatre and the good offices there of Kenneth Alan Taylor and Pat Trueman, "Fur Coat and No Knickers", "One Night Stand" and "Not With a Bang" would never have seen the light of day. I remember all those days of working with the actors and staff at the theatre, from box office girls to backstage electricians, with great fondness. Thanks for all the help."

MIKE HARDING

"The happiest days of my career were at 'the Rep'. I wish that other actresses could have the opportunity that was given to me. What joyous memories I have of the Temperance Hall and the Coliseum. Long may it reign."

DORA BRYAN

"Having met my wife at the Coliseum and brought up two children virtually within its walls, it will always have a place in my heart. Also, I promise you, nowhere in the British Isles will you find such warm, enthusiastic, honest audiences. If they love you, they really let you know . . . If they don't then they will certainly call a spade a shovel.

Here's to another hundred years."

KENNETH ALAN TAYLOR

Kenneth Alan Taylor with David Kossoff in 'Big Night for Shylock', 1968.

"I have many happy memories of my beginnings as an actor at the Coliseum under the gentle care of Douglas Emery who "discovered" me. I hope the Coliseum continues to encourage young actors and to entertain audiences for many more years."

BERNARD CRIBBINS

"This lovely theatre has been such an integral part of my life it's hard to express in a few words my affection for it. I started my career there, met my husband, had my children and brought them up whilst closely involved with it. Oldham is and always has been my home, so whatever I say is going to sound trite. However, thank you for the past and here's to many more successful happy years in the future. Whatever would I do without it!"

JUDITH BARKER

Dora Bryan

"It was at the Coliseum that I was given my first chance to be a professional actor, and as it is almost forty years ago I feel that we both made the right choice. However, full of the arrogance of youth and a pocketful of demob money, I wasn't really particular whether they took me on or not. At that time I was determined to be a stand-up visual comic, fortunately for me they gave me a chance. As a matter of fact I shudder when I think how near Oldham Rep came to turning me down, had they done so, and with every justification, I might now be retired, having spent a boring frustrating life in a cotton mill."

ERIC SYKES

Eric Sykes with President, Frank Hanson on the left and Development Officer Eddie Powell, in 1959.

CASEY'S COURT CIRCUS—1906—INCLUDING THE GREAT CHARLIE CHAPLIN.

COLOSSEUM, Oldham --- MONDAY, 7th DEC.

Introduction

During the week commencing December 7, 1908, Charlie Chaplin was in Oldham performing in a show called "Casey's Court Circus". Even then, at the age of only 19, he was billed as "the great Charlie Chaplin", but as he had been on the stage since the age of six he had had time enough to build up a reputation! The theatre in which he performed was in a little side street off a busy main road. It had been in existence for 22 years and was called the Colosseum. It changed its name to the COLISEUM in 1939, but we shall come to that in due course.

Now 1908 was something of a watershed in the history of popular entertainment in Oldham. It was a year during which two new theatres were built in the town, bringing the total number of theatres up to six. Live theatre – if we include music hall and variety turns like Buffalo Bill's Wild West Show – was probably at its peak of popularity at this time, and its deadly rival, the cinema, was only just beginning to creep in. 1908 saw Brown's Picture House opened in Wallshaw Street – the herald of that great invading crowd of cinemas which, during the next 20 years, would chase away the live theatre from Oldham. These cinemas came in at the rate of about one a year: Dreamland, Mumps, in 1909; Popular Picture Palace, Bridge Street, in 1911; the Kings in 1911; the Palladium in 1913 – and so on into the Twenties and Thirties. Television, of course, which would wound the cinema as deeply as the cinema would wound the theatre, was only a gleam in someone's eye at that time, but John Logie Baird, the television pioneer, was 20 years old in 1908.

So Oldham now possessed six fine theatres:

The Grand, opposite the Star Inn in Union Street, 1908.
The Palace, at the other end of Union Street, 1908. (It eventually became the Odeon Cinema.)
The Empire, Waterloo Street, 1897.
The Colosseum, Fairbottom Street, 1887.
The Gaiety, Union Street, 1868. (Originally the Adelphi, it suffered several changes of name and function.)
The Theatre Royal, Horsedge Street, 1845. (It began life as the Working Man's Hall.)

Now suppose that someone had been asked to bet on which of these would survive as a live theatre to the last decade of the twentieth century. It is quite certain that he would not have put his money on the Colosseum, a wooden building of rather peculiar origins and diverse functions, not all of them theatrical. Almost any of the other five – all good solid buildings – would have seemed the safer bet without any doubt at all. Yet here we are today, approaching the end of the century, and we know now, to our surprise, that the Colosseum has outlasted the rest. The Theatre Royal and the Empire have been demolished; the Palace, which, as the Odeon, survived to be one of the last two cinemas in Oldham, now stands empty; and the Grand and the Gaiety are now, under different names, merely night clubs. So the old Colosseum has not only beaten its theatrical rivals in the survival race, but it has also seen off about 20 cinemas which used to flourish in the Oldham area.

The Colosseum still lives on like a splendid old lady, looking all the better for several face-lifts over the years, and she now celebrates her hundredth birthday. One hundred years old? Well, yes. She has been in Fairbottom Street since 1887 and if she wishes to trim her real age by a few years who will be so churlish as to complain? In a sense she had her origins about a quarter of a mile away. Although the theatre was not actually moved as a whole to Fairbottom Street enough of the timbers and other material from the previous building were used to allow us to claim a fair degree of physical continuity. Her years of renown were spent in Fairbottom Street. There were years of shame, too. For one wicked year she turned her back on the live theatre and yielded herself to Hollywood's intoxicating new form of entertainment: the talking pictures. But it did her no good. Nobody wanted to know her in that role. There followed seven years of destitution. She was left down and out, abandoned, empty and dirty. The story of her rise from the gutter and of the triumphs and struggles of her time of greatness is the theme of this work.

The proscenium, 1986.

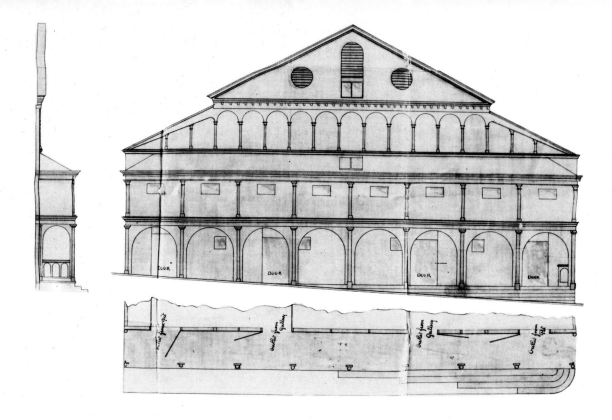

The first fifty years

Above **The façade of the new Colosseum as planned in 1887.**

It all began about 1880 when Oldham, together with other urban and industrial areas of the country, found that things were getting better and more prosperous. (Unfortunately things were not so bright if you worked in agriculture. Cheap foreign food was fine for the town worker but disastrous for the countryman.) Queen Victoria was firmly on the throne, and the British Empire was so arranged that the sun never set on it. The Royal Navy, resting on the laurels of its Nelsonian victories 70 years earlier, ruled the waves, and Britain was the workshop of the world. Most of the worst social consequences of the Industrial Revolution had been cleared up. The cost of living was falling and the real value of wages was steadily increasing. The national scourge of drunkenness among the working classes had begun to ameliorate probably because the working man began to have a wider variety of goods and services available to him. Better public entertainment was one such service and this was destined to grow and proliferate in the decades to come.

In Oldham a Mr. Myers, proprietor of. Myers's Grand American Hippodrome Circus, decided that he needed a permanent home for his show. Myers in 1885 contracted with Thomas Whittaker, a well-known Oldham tradesman, of the carpentery and joinery firm of Emanuel Whittaker in Rochdale Road, Oldham, (still going strong) for the erection of a permanent home for his circus on a site in Henshaw Street. The building was of wood, but it was obviously substantial and well constructed. The story goes that when Thomas Whittaker presented his bill, Mr. Myers was unable to pay it. A court case ensued. Myers claimed breach of contract because Whittaker had failed to complete the circus. He also complained that the stabling provided was inadequate, as a consequence of which one of his lions had died. At the end of May, 1885, judgment was given in Whittaker's favour. And so Thomas Whittaker was left with a new building on his hands with little chance of finding a purchaser for it. After all, what alternative use is there for a wooden circus? It appears that Mr. Whittaker decided to get his money back by going into show business himself. He opened with a Chinese Fair, followed by an equestrian season featuring Dick Turpin's ride to York. Some time later, however, he converted the building into a music hall and rented it to a Francis Westgate. This was not a success. Whittaker then took out a theatre licence and began to put on stage plays, with Stephen Wall as his theatre manager. This new enterprise proved to be popular, and all seemed set for a prosperous future until Oldham Town Council put an obstacle in his path. It was the Council's intention to build a market hall on Henshaw Street, taking in the site on which the theatre stood. The magistrates would therefore grant Whittaker a theatre licence for only three months at a time. This, of course, made it almost impossible to provide a viable theatre programme, and it was not long before Thomas Whittaker decided that he had had enough of Henshaw Street. Obviously there is no business like show business for giving someone a life full

Holebottom Colliery, later to be the site of Whittaker's new theatre.

of stress, and Thomas Whittaker was not the first, nor the last, to find that out.

His plan was to find a new site, dismantle the theatre and re-erect it on its new location. The site he obtained was in Fairbottom Street, the approach road to an old colliery and just off one of the main roads of the town, Yorkshire Street. The new site was bought cheaply, but it was well placed. The Theatre Royal was adjacent to it and, ten years later, the Empire Theatre would be built only 100 yards away.

There were about 50 collieries in Oldham in the middle of the nineteenth century, but by the end of the century many of them had been worked out. Today there is none left. In 1887 the town was littered with old colliery workings and 100 years later the shafts still cause trouble to builders. A glance at the photograph of the Fairbottom Street area taken before the theatre moved there will reveal at once why the site was cheap. Even by nineteenth century standards it was a run-down area. The Holebottom Colliery ceased operation in 1880, and the site had been derelict for seven years.

Here it was that Thomas Whittaker erected his theatre, the Colosseum, in 1887. We are fortunate in having the account of an eye-witness of the birth of the new theatre: Walter Wall, the son of Whittaker's theatre manager, Stephen Wall.

"Looking back on the early days of the Colosseum, recollections of happenings in those far

off times come crowding back on one's memory. Selecting a few at random, perhaps my earliest recollection is seeing stacks (or do they call them "stands") of timber in Emanuel Whittaker's yard in Rochdale Road, and being told they were to be used in the building of a new theatre. Later, I saw the baulks of timber go into position in Fairbottom Street, once the approach to an old colliery. Eventually the roof went on with very little time to spare before the theatre opening.

Being built entirely of wood, the theatre was suspect from a fire danger point of view, and opinions differed greatly as to whether it could be used as a theatre with safety. Specially-designed spring-steel bars which operated on pressure from inside were fitted to wide exit doors which made it possible to empty the theatre within two minutes. In those days the pit alone would hold nearly a thousand – in fact, 999 paid for admission to one Saturday matinee performance of a pantomime.

All the wood used in the building was fire-proofed, and a good advertisement was obtained by publicising the fact that scrap ends of the timber were of no use as chips for fire-lighting. Even the Fire Brigade could not light a fire with them. I remember them trying. On all day bills and programmes appeared the words, "The Safe Theatre", and also a statement by the chief of the Manchester Fire Brigade that a wooden staircase was safer in a fire than a stone one. Gas was used as an illuminant and the limelights for following the artists were truly "limelights". The gas used for them was produced on the premises, and the "limes" shaped and drilled in a workshop under the stage. They were worked from "lime shelves", two on each side behind the proscenium, and from the wings, the simple burners or mixers being enclosed in big clumsy boxes.

The footlights were of gas (not incandescent mantles) with a pilot light at each end. Sometimes the lights would not run along and had to be encouraged by stage hands blowing the flame along from one burner to the next. There was a contrivance by which coloured glass could be raised between the footlights and the stage. These glass screens were amber, red and green.

On the back wall of the stage was a huge frame on which canvas was stretched and painted into scenery, the scenic artists working from a bridge which they raised or lowered at will."

Coliseum plans 1837.

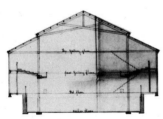
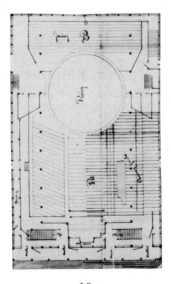
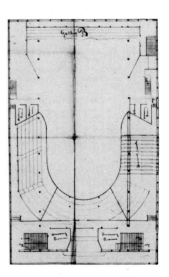

Although Thomas Whittaker had stumbled into show business by accident, it is evident that he became deeply interested in it. Apart from the fact that he kept the theatre for nearly 20 years there is also the evidence that, when he came to transfer the building from Henshaw Street to Fairbottom Street, he was already knowledgeable and enthusiastic enough to be able to introduce some quite revolutionary improvements. The floor of the auditorium could be raised and lowered by a mechanism perhaps designed by Whittaker himself. By this means the auditorium floor could be brought up level with the stage, thus providing an extensive flat area for use as a ballroom or exhibition hall. The new Colosseum was, above all things, adaptable. Whatever the public wanted, whatever was profitable to provide, the new theatre could accommodate it – drama or opera; grand ball or commercial bazaar; circus, music hall or pantomime. Thomas Whittaker had learned a great deal about the entertainment industry in a very short time.

On June 10, 1887, Queen Victoria completed 50 years of her reign. The Golden Jubilee celebrations were observed in every town and village in the country, for the old Queen had become a popular and much-loved monarch. The outburst of republican sentiments which had occurred earlier in the century and the public dissatisfaction expressed at her prolonged mourning for Prince Albert had been forgotten. Oldham celebrated with the rest of the nation and it was a happy chance that the new Colosseum was able to reopen on that particular day with a presentation of Culeen's Circus, including animals, Red Indians and trapeze artistes. The new theatre, said a contemporary account in the Oldham Evening Chronicle, is "a magnificent building, the largest of the kind in Oldham, fitted up with every convenience which the thought of experienced men can suggest for comfort. The centre seats of the dress circle, upholstered in Utrecht velvet, rise gradually from the front, so that those behind can not only see over the heads of their male neighbours, but over the tallest feminine headgear that fashion can devise. The exits from the pit are at the side, and some idea of the attention given to this all-important matter may be gathered from the fact that it is claimed to be possible to clear three thousand people out of the building in two minutes".

A Colosseum playbill of 1890.

The Colosseum in 1913.

The first staff of the Working Department of the Colosseum, 1888.

The theatre also had an early form of air-conditioning, which provided cold, heated or perfumed air.

So the Colosseum started upon its first 100 years. Thomas Whittaker, of course, for all his suddenly acquired flair for the entertainment business, did have the family joinery firm to run. After a few years he let the theatre to a Mr. Ernest Dottridge, and, later, in February, 1903, he sold the theatre to Joseph Ball, a local steeplejack and very colourful character, who was acting on behalf of Peter Yates of the Yates's Wine Lodges. The transaction was agreed in a steam-tram going down the Rochdale road. The price was £4,000. Three years later, in 1906, the Market Hall was opened – 20 years after its proposed erection caused the Colosseum to be shifted!

The end of the nineteenth century brought something of a renaissance of English drama. Pinero, Wilde, Jones, Shaw, Galsworthy were writing plays immensely superior to the crude melodramas of earlier years, and the Manchester Gaiety Theatre, under the redoubtable Miss Horniman, was launching playwrights like Stanley Houghton. But we must not deceive ourselves

A poster advertising the Colosseum's production of "Two Little Drummer Boys" outside the Carriers Arms, Shaw, in 1900.

about the tastes of Oldham audiences in those years. George Rowell in his introduction to a collection of nineteenth century plays wrote:

"No other era, mediaeval, Elizabethan, or modern, has been so utterly dominated by the demands of the masses. 'Entertain us or be gone' was the dictate of the Victorian audience, and the entertainers, whether actors, singers, acrobats, painters, machinists or performers of any kind, including performers with the pen, heeded that voice or starved."

Walter Wall's reminiscences tell us of the astonishing mixture of plays and other entertainments put on at the Colosseum.

"In those days the stages of most provincial theatres were occupied by travelling companies and there was tremendous rivalry between the Theatre Royal and the Colosseum managements to get the best of these travelling companies. Occasionally 'stock' companies came and stayed three or four weeks. The great event of the year, however, was panto season, which opened on Christmas Eve and ran usually for six weeks.

Great shows these pantos were – by any standards. Home-made, too, in that the 'book' was written locally and all props and scenery made and painted at the theatre specially for each panto production. The chorus and crowds and show girls were mostly locals, and some really good bright shows were produced. Emphasis was placed on good singing. In one of these pantos the Fairy Queen was played by a Carl Rosa prima donna, the Demon King by a leading operatic baritone, and the Second Girl by an Italian-trained singer who went straight from the Colosseum panto to play leads at Covent Garden.

Strong drama was the main attraction during the rest of the year, interspersed by grand opera and comedy, and once a year a week of Shakespeare played by Osmond Tearle's company. That truly great actor, the father of the late Sir Godfrey Tearle, was a great favourite with Oldham audiences, and I still think no actor has played 'King Lear', 'Coriolanus', or for that matter 'Othello', better than did Osmond Tearle in his prime.

The Arthur Rousby Opera Company came once a year and played to packed houses every show. The operas were the usual run of operas then popular 'Il Travotore', 'Carmen', 'Faust', 'Lohengrin', 'Cavaliera Rusticana' and 'Pagliacci' (always on a Friday), and always great discussion as to whether on Saturday night 'The Bohemian Girl' or 'Maritana' should be put on.

Of the plays, melodrama most melodramatic. I remember best 'The Grip of Iron', with Sam Livesey, a forbear of Roger Livesey; 'The Face at the Window'; 'East Lynne', of course; 'Is Life Worth Living', in which a real steamroller was used and came within inches of flattening out the heroine lying in a dead faint in its track; 'The Still Alarm', in which a real fire engine was drawn across the stage by two horses which dashed from their stalls and placed themselves under trick harness which automatically fastened; and that really fine play, 'The Silver King'."

Now we are entering the early years of the great era of cinema as the dominant mass entertainment. However the advent of the film did not present an immediate threat to the theatre managers of the day, who treated it simply as an addition to the richly varied programmes they were in the habit of providing. A mixture of silent films and live variety acts became common and the Colosseum joined

A Colosseum playbill of 1928.

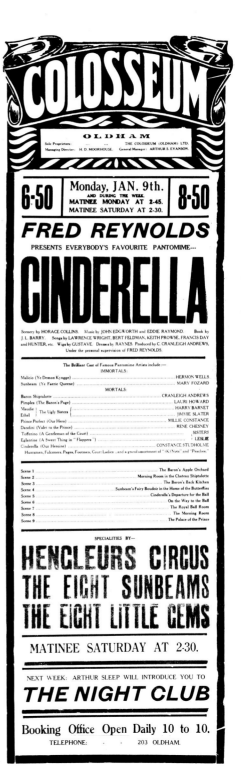

the trend in 1911. In 1918, it was bought by Dobie's Electric Theatres. This mix of film and live acts survived intermittently until as late as the Second World War and many people may still remember going to cinemas offering a double film programme with jugglers and acrobats performing between the films.

One of the well-known companies of entertainers to visit the Colosseum was Fred Karno's Company, including Charlie Chaplin, offering such shows as "Early Birds", "Gaol Birds", and "Mumming Birds". As a contrast, on Sunday nights, political meetings used to be held in the Colosseum. Its auditorium has resounded to the oratory of such as Lord Emmott, Lloyd George, Walter Runciman, Ramsay Macdonald, J. R. Clynes, Victor Grayson and Duff Cooper.

For a decade the Colosseum survived beside the growing popularity of the film, though other theatres in the town were, one by one, converting into cinemas. The end for the Colosseum was very near.

In 1927 the actor Al Jolson appeared in "The Jazz Singer" and in it Jolson was heard to talk and to sing: the "talkies" had arrived. From then on the rate of conversion of theatres to cinemas increased but, even so, the Colosseum held out until March, 1931. It was advertising itself as

The Oldham Colosseum
The natural talkie theatre

This was meant to imply that on its stage one could see and hear actors speaking natural speech. In spite of this the audiences made it quite clear that what they wanted was "talkies" not plays, and so, on Saturday, March 4, 1931, a 44-year period of live theatre in the Colosseum ended with a performance of "The Novelty Box".

On the following Monday this notice appeared in the local press:

Oldham Colosseum
The super 'talkie' theatre

**Closed for the installation of talkies.
Reopening Monday next, March 23, with a
wonder programme.**

The "super all-talking programme" with which it reopened included the film "Two Worlds", with Randle Ayrton, John Longden and Norah Baring – "a drama of inter-marriage between two races: a conflict of hate and love". Later that year the stage effects of the theatre were sold off in 200 lots and fetched about £350. The triumph of the silver screen seemed complete; the live theatre was believed to be finished.

In spite of this, the Colosseum's flirtation with the new form of mass entertainment lasted only nine months and with the showing of "The Bat Whispers" ("the greatest talking mystery thriller of all times"), the Colosseum closed its doors to the public on Saturday, January 2, not to reopen for seven years. The great trade depression of the thirties had arrived. The American stock market crash of 1929 had started a gale which howled through the USA and Europe leaving a trail of economic ruin and shabby hordes of unemployed men. The bill for the Great War could no longer be evaded.

An industrial town like Oldham was bound to suffer and the slump hit it hard. Property values fell and a Mr. Crossman, rather unwisely perhaps, bought the Colosseum very cheaply indeed and began to make many alterations to it with the idea of creating a comfortable modern cinema. Unfortunately the cinema licence for the building had lapsed, and when Mr. Crossman applied for a new one, he found that the Watch Committee was applying more rigorous standards and old wooden buildings converted into cinemas did not find much favour. He made two attempts to obtain a licence and failed on both occasions. This was obviously the end of the road for the Colosseum, which was left empty and, as the grim years of the Depression wore on, it stood in Fairbottom Street dirty and dilapidated – a silent, dark shell of a failed theatre.

Resurrection

When, early in 1936, the Grand Theatre closed its doors and proceeded to transform itself into the Gaumont Super-Cinema (complete with wonder organ), live theatre in Oldham appeared to be finally dead. The other theatres had either closed, like the Colosseum, or had become cinemas, like the Grand. The same process was occurring in nearly every town in the country and now, 50 years later, few towns possess a live theatre and in many towns all the cinemas have disappeared, too. Oldham is one of the few towns which does still boast a living and lively theatre. The credit for this must be spread over hundreds of people who have worked for and supported the theatre for the last 50 years but the man who undoubtedly planted the seed in 1936 was Joe Holroyd. He it was who flushed out a group of determined and enthusiastic theatre-lovers by placing an advertisement in the Oldham Evening Chronicle appealing to people who cared deeply about repertory theatre to get together and do something positive to keep it going in Oldham. As a result of the advertisement a meeting was held in the house of Miss Phyllis Bennett, a local teacher, and things began to happen. A local writer, Armitage Owen, provided some money and a room was hired at Greenacres Co-operative Hall in which a public meeting was held. Out of this the Oldham Playgoers' Club was born. The club, according to one of its early documents, was for lovers of drama and the theatre, and its policy was to encourage the public to display a greater interest in the repertory movement generally and, in particular, the local theatre.

The editor of the club's magazine looked back on these events two years later: he referred to the small band of young people who lived in the age of cinemas and were not satisfied and who went on to create the club.

"Without a theatre in the town, with no plays to attend, the little band resolved to keep alive the drama and support the living theatre in Oldham. You

may smile, others did. They held meetings on Sunday evenings in dance halls – these were the only places where a room was available at a reasonable rent.

Then came the good news: 'Rep coming back to the Theatre Royal'. Wholeheartedly the Playgoers Club supported. Members of T. C. Williamson's Company addressed the club meetings. All seemed well. Then came another blow: 'In a fortnight this theatre will be changing over to variety'. Dismayed but undaunted the Playgoers rallied and decided to petition for the return of the Rep. They stood long hours in sleet and snow collecting signatures; they were removed from the theatre for publicly protesting against the departure of the Repertory Company . . . The Repertory went."

The date was December, 1937. Joe Holroyd, himself, looking back on those days tells us:

"A Playgoers' Club is a society of people who enjoy going to plays. Such a club was formed in Oldham to support the Lawrence-Williamson Repertory Company at the Theatre Royal.

Roger Williams, the Theatre Club's first Producer.

"Previous, to this, as a young man of 16, I had bombarded the local press with letters about the theatre, signing myself "Twelve Interested Repertory Fans". I thought this powerful nom de plume would merit immediate attention, and it seemed to do the trick, for the Oldham Chronicle printed every one of them.

Later, when the commercially-minded management of the Theatre Royal suggested we moved to premises smaller than their theatre, we took refuge in Billington's Dancing Academy. During our stay there one might have seen a group of strolling players presenting scenes from Shakespeare in bizarre surroundings far more unusual than those conjured up by the theatre-in-the-round of today!

Soon the time came when repertory vanished from Oldham, and it was then that we went into action which was to prove that we were indeed playgoers worthy of the name. With a membership of not more than 90 we canvassed the entire district, rented the Temperance Hall in Horsedge Street, and set about turning it into a theatre."

Many people in the town thought that the foundation of a Playgoers' Club in Oldham in those days was ridiculous enough, but that this club should set up its own theatre and engage its own repertory company – well, it seemed time to call in the men with the white coats and strait-jackets! Undeterred, these inspired lunatics went on to equip the Temperance Hall with 217 seats bought cheaply from Miss Horniman's Gaiety Theatre in Manchester. The seating was set off tastefully with a strip of coconut matting down each side on the cold wooden floor. Enthusiastic volunteers distempered the dirty walls. The hall was not raked but, as H. C. Loader, one of the pioneers, tells us:

"In their amateur ignorance the officials considered that the raking of the stage was essential, and the local joiner who did the job saw to it that they certainly got what they asked for!"

Meanwhile the club engaged Roger Williams to bring his company to Oldham and an application for a theatre licence was submitted to the local magistrates who promptly turned it down. The Temperance Hall, even with coconut matting strips on the floor and nice clean walls, fell far below the standard required by the regulations governing the granting of a public theatre licence. The club turned to its legal friends and found a way to avoid this impasse. Were the theatre to be available only to members of a private club and their friends, the licence regulations would not apply. So the Oldham Repertory Theatre Club was swiftly formed with 200 foundation members – each paying ten shillings (50p) – and a drive was made to recruit 1,000 ordinary members paying 2s. 6d. (12½p) a year. One really has to marvel at the speed with which these people got things done. On Saturday, January 31, 1938, the makeshift theatre threw open its doors on a dark and stormy night and waited anxiously to present Bernard Shaw's "Arms and the Man". An audience did turn up in spite of the weather. One of the founder members, Dr. Watson, later described by Miss Bennett as "a kindly old soul", provided a half-pound box of chocolates for each woman in the audience, and he also lent the spoons for the audience to stir their coffee in the interval. Professional theatre was back in Oldham.

By April the membership of the new club had reached 2,000 and a club magazine was launched. The time came when the "House Full" board began to be used. There were queues before the doors opened. And a new play each week.

The sane and sober people of Oldham began to change their opinion: perhaps these crazy Playgoers were not as daft as they appeared. The first year was an undoubted success, and it was gratifyingly evident that the Temperance Hall was not large enough to contain all the Oldhamers who enjoyed weekly repertory. In 1939 the Club launched its most audacious scheme: to rent and to restore the derelict Colosseum and to move their repertory theatre there. The sane and sober people of Oldham reverted to their previous opinion: the Playgoers were obviously quite mad.

It was becoming increasingly obvious by the beginning of 1939 that war with Germany was inevitable. Our country was rearming fast. Already every person had been issued with a gas mask. It is often forgotten how people in the thirties imagined the outbreak of another European war. Nearly everyone – and this included the government and its advisers – expected devastating air raids upon our big towns with high explosive and incendiary bombs, and with poison gas. The Manchester conurbation appeared to offer an obvious target for such an onslaught. What a time to choose to open a failed and derelict theatre in Oldham!

Mr. W. R. Peake, the first chairman of the Oldham Repertory Theatre Club, looking back 25 years later, wrote:

"At the close of the second performance of 'Lot's Wife' on July 15th, 1939, the audience and company sang 'Auld Lang Syne' as the curtain came down on the last show in the Temperance Hall, and on the following Monday the Club opened its doors at the Coliseum with 'Poison Pen'.

Some months before this, the Committee of Management had taken a bold step. The Colosseum, as the name was then spelt, was not in use. The Treasurer of the Club at that time was Mr. Jack Taylor. He, and I as Chairman, envisaged the possibility of the Rep being transferred there. It was a great surprise to the Committee when the idea was put before them and we all went to view the theatre.

Many alterations and additions were needed, and the funds of the Club were indeed meagre, but the Temperance Hall was becoming too small to accommodate the members, so something had to be done. The Committee decided to acquire the Colosseum, and the lease and agreement were signed on May 23, 1939, and the name was changed to Coliseum.

The floor of the auditorium was one expanse of bare earth, which had to be covered with wooden flooring. Seats had to be erected, a proscenium and stage built, wiring and electrical equipment to be installed. All this work was done by Mr. Armitage of Lees, who attended to the timber work, and Mr. James Fazakerley of the James Engineering Co., who attended to the electrical work. Both were kindly disposed to the Rep, and waited patiently to be paid. The total cost was just over £700. Both accounts were paid in under two years.

Excitement and anxiety prevailed as opening day approached. To think that a few people from all walks of life – all amateurs in the business of theatre management – should embark on such an undertaking. Was it any wonder we were anxious?"

The Coliseum in 1939.

The members of the club had lost none of their former drive, determination and speed at getting things done. To sign the lease on May 23 and to have the theatre ready by July 15 was a remarkable achievement.

Mrs. Mabel Hill, founder member of the club, acted as House Manageress from 1938 until 1943, organising the voluntary front-of-house staff. She described the move to the new premises:

"During the early part of our second year speculation was rife. 'Have you heard? We might be moving to the Colosseum.' A real theatre at last! Volunteers were called for, and some of the usherettes became Mrs. Mops. Members of the company joined us, husbands and fathers joined with the Committee to clear away six years of dust and dirt – not a very inspiring sight. But what is this? Let joy be unconfined. We now have a foyer with a separate box office. This is plush living indeed! Upstairs to the circle, and, glory be, the old centre circle is intact, with the original seats and real carpet between the rows. Columbus himself could not have been more joyous."

Douglas Emery, Producer, 1940–1950.

That is how the old Colosseum was reborn, and, as Saul the Pharisee became Paul the Christian, so the Colosseum arose from its dirt and dereliction as the COLISEUM. On the night of July 15, 1939, with war only seven weeks away, the Mayor and Mayoress of Oldham, councillors and local dignitaries, and proud members of the Oldham Repertory Theatre Club, watched the first play of the old/new theatre's second 50 years.

Although the old building had suffered several major changes since 1887, the basic structure of wood was still there, and, indeed, remained until 1965. During its cinema period it had acquired an ugly projection box perched over the façade of the theatre, and the architecture of the back-stage area had also been considerably mutilated. The stage area had been demolished, since the use of the building as a cinema demanded nothing but a silver screen across the proscenium. The area which had formerly been back-stage and dressing rooms was also demolished, leaving an open area between the back of the theatre and the end of Bartlam Place. The row of dressing rooms on the north side of this area were originally stables, used for performing animals during the building's use as a circus. When the Repertory Club took over, instead of rebuilding the stage, they cut the auditorium in two, using the front part as the stage area, which accounts for the awkward way the side circle seats run straight into the proscenium. It is certain that it would not have been granted a theatre licence had one been applied for, but as with the Temperance Hall, the Coliseum was a private theatre used by members of the ORTC and their friends, and so the regulations did not apply.

War, in due course, did break out, but, to universal surprise and relief, death and devastation did not rain down from the skies, and, even when the air raids were launched upon Britain, deadly and destructive though they were, they did not match the awful shape of pre-war fears. Oldham, indeed, found itself regarded as a safe area! And in this haven of security the Coliseum prospered. Membership of the Repertory Club at one time soared above 20,000. Great London companies visited the town and the theatre was more than once

Left **The Old Vic Company are entertained in the Mayor's Parlour, 1940.**

Below **A production of "Painted Sparrows", 1942.**

Robert Newton and Dora Bryan rehearse "Semi-Private", 1946.

_____Rehearsals in 1946.

host to the Sadlers Wells Opera Company, the Old Vic Company and the Ballet Rambert. Members of the armed forces in uniform were allowed into the theatre performances without payment. House full notices were frequently displayed, particularly on Saturday nights. The seating capacity at that time was 738.

Eric Landless-Turner, the Club's Treasurer wrote in the programme for the week commencing November 19, 1945:

"During and after December 3rd week the free admission of troops will be confined to Monday and Wednesday evenings and to the matinees. We feel proud to think that throughout the war we have been probably the only theatre in England that has given unquestioned free admission to anyone in H.M. Forces. When Oldham was full of troops it was quite common to see from a hundred to a hundred and fifty of them at a performance and their appreciation was most gratifying."

There is no doubt that the Coliseum built up a national reputation during the war years. Eminent members of the theatrical world visited Oldham and were astonished to find that this rather dingy industrial town not only possessed a comfortable theatre but also that the theatre attracted thousands of Oldham people. The Coliseum was the theatrical success story of the decade. That very popular weekly, Picture Post, published an enthusiastic article by Antonia White on March 16, 1946: "Oldham runs its own theatre". Three years later, on March 23, 1949, an account of the Oldham Rep written by Eric Turner appeared in the "News Chronicle". The Coliseum was news.

In his article Eric Turner attributed the success of the Rep (as the theatre was known in the town) to these facts:

"1. Oldham's is a non-profit making theatre, and so good plays can be seen at a price that everyone can afford. (Admission is 1s.9d. for any seat in the house and 1s.0d. for the juniors.)

"Dear Octopus", 1942. Dora Bryan and Bernard Cribbins were amongst the cast.

2.   Apart from 15 professional artists and five paid workers, the theatre is run by eager volunteers. (80 local girls work on a nightly rota as ushers and serve refreshments, bringing in a yearly profit of £1,000.)

3.   Plays of entertainment are produced and 'educational' plays are not crammed on the audience, but presented at about one a month.

4.   The people of Oldham want a theatre."

However, it should also be added that there were other reasons for the success of the theatre. Eric Turner himself was a very hard-working and energetic treasurer, and Douglas Emery, who was the producer from 1940 until 1950, certainly gave the theatre-hungry public a programme of plays and a quality of production that had them literally queuing up each week. These two, ably supported by a vigorous committee, provided the drive to keep the theatre going.

The club had rented the Coliseum since 1939. In 1942 a Building Fund had been started and plans laid for the building of a new and larger post-war theatre. (The young ORTC was never afraid to have audacious ambitions.) However, the lease on the theatre ran out in 1946 and this presented the club with its first big crisis, because the landlord refused to renew the lease and, instead, offered to sell the theatre to the club for £15,000. Negotiations lowered the price to £11,000 and the club, using its Building Fund and an interest-free loan from the bank of £3,000, eventually acquired the theatre and the surrounding land.

One might look upon this as a fitting conclusion to the first period of the new club's history. The war had brought the theatre success, national fame and financial stability. Now it had to face the cold winds of the post-war world as the owner of a much-altered, but still a basically wooden, theatre, 60 years old.

24

Walter Greenwood, author of "Love on the Dole", shows actor Robert Newton (with stick) the sights of Oldham, 1946.

The Oldham Repertory Theatre
Club Committee, 1946.
The President, Mrs. Florence Jagger,
then aged 82, is on the left.

Above & Left **Photographs of Douglas
Emery and Company in 1946.**

The war was over, the armed forces were being demobilised, and the new Labour government, under Clement Attlee, was struggling to rebuild Britain. The long, bitter winter of 1947 was hard to endure: supplies of food, fuel and electricity were low. It was a miserable time. In the January of that harsh winter, during a performance of "Macbeth", a bizarre and disturbing tragedy occurred on the stage of the Coliseum. In the course of the fight between Macduff and Macbeth in the final scene, the actor Harold Norman, playing the leading role, was accidentally stabbed by Anthony Oakley, playing Macduff. The injured man staggered into the wings and remained there. Douglas Emery said to him, "Go and take your curtain call, Harold," not realising until he saw blood on the other's costume that anything was wrong. Harold Norman was rushed to hospital. The prop sword had penetrated 4 in. into his abdomen, but the seriousness of the wound was not immediately apparent and peritonitis set in. Harold Norman died on February 27 in hospital. Two hundred people attended his funeral and the theatre was closed for the day. "Macbeth", of course, has always been regarded as an unlucky play by members of the theatrical profession – things tend to go wrong when it is put on. This stroke of ill luck was an ominous beginning to the new era.

A formidable backlog of repairs, necessary alterations and replacements had been accumulating during the war years when, of course, there was an acute shortage of labour and materials. New seating was installed in 1948, which resulted in the number of available seats in the theatre being reduced by 100. The old Temperance Hall, which was being used by the company as a workshop and store for the theatre, was found to be unsafe. The backstage accommodation in the theatre itself was cramped and unsatisfactory. As the decade ended a new crisis for the club began to develop. Its main ingredients were to become uncomfortably familiar to the club members as they reappeared again and again during the next 25 years.

It is obvious from the way the Oldham Repertory Theatre Club was born that its leading members were people with drive, energy, strong views and a determination to get their way. They needed to be like that to create and to sustain a repertory theatre in

---

INJURED BY DAGGER IN STAGE DUEL

REPERTORY PLAYER IN SERIOUS CONDITION

MAJOR OPERATION PERFORMED

Mr. Harold Norman, who is in Oldham Royal Infirmary following an accident on the Coliseum stage when he was wounded with a dagger, is seriously ill and yesterday underwent a major operation. He was playing the title role in this week's production by the Oldham Repertory Company of "Macbeth," a production which marks the company's ninth birthday.

The wound occurred during the battle between Macbeth and Macduff, played by Antony Oakley, on Thursday night. The battle was a realistic one, the two men, who are close friends, fighting first with swords and then with daggers.

At first it was thought that the wound was not serious, and it was described as "superficial," but yesterday a specialist found that Mr Norman was injured internally.

Exaggerated reports have been circulated of women in the audience screaming and of the audience having stood to cheer Macbeth's fine show of agony at the end of the play.

The truth is however, that the audience was not aware that anything serious had happened. Mr Douglas Emery, the Repertory Company producer, told a "Chronicle" reporter that after he fell Mr. Norman crawled off the stage. At the final curtain the producer came on to say that Mr. Norman had been hurt but, he thought, he would be all right in a few minutes.

Mr. Emery, who was standing in the wings at the time of the accident waiting to ring down the final curtain, said "Harold had his back to the audience at the time, and I think he must have run on to Mr. Oakley's dagger. He crawled off the stage, and I thought he was winded. Then I found he was injured and would be unable to make his curtain speech, so I told the audience he was hurt."

The stage manager, Mr. Arthur Hall, who was playing Banquo, took over the part of Macbeth last night.

Mr. Norman as Iago in the company's production of "Othello."

Antony Oakley

Oldham. It is equally obvious that people with these excellent qualities often set up a backwash which upsets lesser mortals, and, moreover, they do tend to fall out with each other. Add in actors and actresses, who, so I am told, sometimes have a teeny tendency to be temperamental, and you have a potentially effervescent mixture.

As early in the club's history as 1938 a small cloud could be observed on the horizon. Joe Holroyd himself, who by then was the club's secretary, resigned from the committee because he was not in agreement with its policy. Fortunately he remained a loyal member of the club and a staunch supporter of the Coliseum, which, I am very happy to record, he remains to this day.

By 1950 large storm clouds were gathering. Douglas Emery, who had been producing successful plays for the Rep Theatre since 1940, began to clash with the committee. Club members began to take sides. Hard words were exchanged. Things became so heated and so tense that an opposition group was set up, the Oldham Repertory Friends' Association, with the express purpose of wresting control of the club from the hands of the existing committee. Accusations of extravagant expenditure, dictatorial attitudes and neglect of bad backstage conditions were being aired in public. In September, Douglas Emery resigned because he no longer agreed with the policy of the committee of the club. This resignation proved to be the flame which set alight the whole undergrowth of discontent, and the correspondence page of the Oldham Evening Chronicle exploded with letters of complaint, counter-complaint, accusation and counter-accusation. A demand was made, supported by a petition, for a special meeting of the club to consider a motion of no confidence in the committee. The meeting was arranged for January 3, 1951 in the Hill Stores. One thousand members turned up. The event was noisy, prolonged and disorderly, but in the end, by an overwhelming show of hands, the vote of no confidence was passed. A subsequent ballot and a lively annual meeting in August put the nominees of the Repertory Friends firmly in control. "It will now be possible," said R. H. Mellor, the new chairman, "to attain some measure of stability." The God of Theatres heard

Guy Vaesen, Producer, 1950–1951.

this and laughed. Two weeks later Douglas Emery resigned again. The club members rushed into their appropriate trenches and war broke out once more. What had gone wrong?

The crisis of the previous year had occurred because of the resignation of Douglas Emery as producer, and the rebels had his reinstatement high on their list. However, another producer, Guy Vaesen, had been appointed before the rebels took over and he had a contract which expired on August 13, 1951. Douglas Emery was brought back into the temporary position of manager and secretary with the obvious understanding that the producer's job would return to him on the expiry of Vaesen's contract.

However, Douglas Emery believed that the time had come to appoint a producer-manager. The Committee disagreed. "Too onerous a burden for one man," they said. The upshot was that Emery refused the offer of the post of Director of Productions. The Committee took this to be the end of the matter and appointed Miss Yvonne Le Dain as producer and Mr. Harry Lomax, a member of the acting staff, as assistant producer. More trouble flared up, but the committee won the support of another vociferous meeting.

Renovations to the Temperance Hall, 1952.

Behind most of the periodical rows which broke out in the course of the club's history, there was one particular issue which rumbled round and round like a summer storm, never really exhausting itself with a few great crashes of thunder and lightning, but continually flickering and muttering on the horizon. This was the old "popular" versus "cultural" argument. Should the Rep put on a programme of trusted and tried comedies, romances and thrillers which were guaranteed to bring in the Oldham audiences, or should the aim be to introduce new works, old classics and plays with a social or political content, which, said the opponents of this line of thought, were guaranteed to keep the theatre half empty. The problem was complicated by the fact that the club theatre was exempt from entertainment tax, but had to present a percentage of cultural plays in order to keep its exemption. Obviously some mixture of the two groups was the best course. It was the exact composition of the mix that kept the controversy going.

Guy Vaesen, the producer during 1951, was obviously trying to move the theatre off the diet of popular, lightweight drama. The Oldham Chronicle's review of the year commented:

"While all the trouble has been simmering, Mr. Guy Vaesen, an unfortunate victim of circumstances, has been going about his work as though nothing were afoot. It is noticeable that during 1951 the Repertory Club has produced more non-commercial plays than in recent years. When one talks of non-commercial work, one really means the productions which might be looked favourably upon by the Customs and Excise in terms of continuing to allow the Club freedom from entertainments tax.

There comes to mind, then, ten productions during the year which come under that loose term non-commercial: 'St. Joan', 'Death of a Salesman', 'The Knight of the Burning Pestle', 'The Merchant of Venice', 'The Springtime of Others', 'The Double Dealer', 'The Young Swallows', 'Death of a Rat', 'Top of the Ladder', 'Mrs. Warren's Profession'. One might add to the list the forthcoming production of '1066 and All That' (certainly a difficult show for weekly repertory)."

With the failure of the vote of no confidence in the committee and with the meeting's support of the committee's action in accepting the resignation of Douglas Emery, all the steam went out of the opposition's campaign and the club settled down to face the real problems of the 1950s. Although Yvonne Le Dain's contract was to expire at the end of January, 1952, she left in November, 1951, by mutual agreement with the club and the associate producer, Harry Lomax, took over with the title of Director of Productions. Announcing this, the club said:

"This appointment means that he will be responsible for the artistic direction of the theatre and consequently will have more authority than has previously been vested in our producer."

Harry Lomax proved to be the second of the four producers who were in that position long enough to stamp their personality on the theatre. He survived until 1959 when the club endured yet another outbreak of civil war.

The annual general meeting of 1952 was told that, for the previous five years, expenses had increased at a greater rate than income, and something had to be done to bring these two into balance for the future. The club tackled the problem with characteristic energy: economies were pursued and income was increased. At the same time the club was able to carry out a number of structural improvements. The Temperance Hall was extensively repaired; the old stables at the back of the theatre were demolished to allow for an extension to the dressing rooms; new stage lighting and a new proscenium arch were installed. It was evident that the committee, following the best traditions of the club, was determined to meet its problems by coming out fighting. A fund-raising pamphlet was issued in 1954, "The Future Depends on You". It told the story of the birth of the Oldham Playgoers and of the Oldham Repertory Theatre Club, and of the opening of the theatre in the Temperance Hall. It described the early history of the Colosseum Theatre and of its rebirth as the Coliseum. And it put forward plans for a new, bigger and better equipped Coliseum of the future.

By the end of 1954 the Coliseum appeared to be back on course and the club's treasurer was able to announce a net profit for the year. The theatre was filling 60% of its seats on average, but the annual meeting was warned that the vision of a new theatre would be a mirage if that figure were not increased to 75%.

Another milestone was reached on Monday, December 2, 1957, when the Rep put on its 1,000th production, which, very fittingly, was Bernard Shaw's "Arms and the Man", the play with which the Temperance Hall Theatre opened in 1938. The club paused for a nostalgic look back at its own history. It had much to be proud about. Against all the odds it had brought repertory back to Oldham. It had picked the old Colosseum out of the dust and set it up again as a live and lively theatre with a national reputation. Many actors prominent on West End stages or on film or television, had their early careers with the Oldham Rep: Dora Bryan, Bernard Cribbins, Eric Sykes, Frank Middlemass and many others. Celebrated actors had appeared on the Coliseum stage: Wendy Hiller, Flora Robson, Frederick Valk, Robert Newton, Marius Goring,

A production for United Nations' Week, 1954, "Mine Hostess". Harry Lomax is on the extreme left.

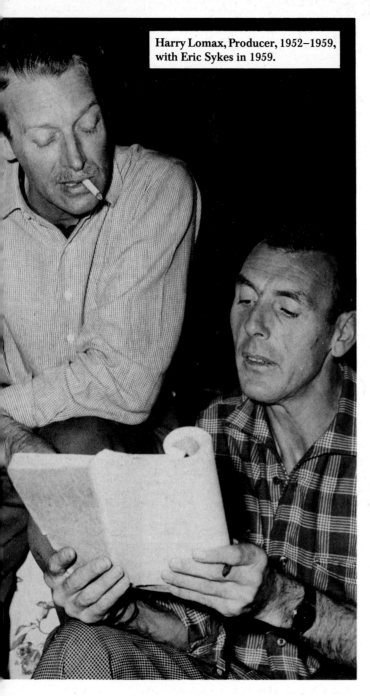

Harry Lomax, Producer, 1952–1959, with Eric Sykes in 1959.

Nova Pilbeam, Claude Hulbert, Thora Hird.

On the following Wednesday 61 of the surviving founder members of the Oldham Repertory Theatre Club were present as invited guests at the performance of the play, and Miss Phyllis Bennett, the only person to have held continuous office in the club since its inception, made what she frankly called a nostalgic and sentimental speech. She reminded her hearers that the first committee had conceived the ambition, still not dead, to buy the Gaumont (originally the Grand Theatre) some day and turn it back again into a theatre. As we have noted before, the founders of the club were never afraid of big ideas!

Eighteen months later the euphoria generated by the 1,000th production was swept away by another storm of quarrels, resignations, petitions and falling box office receipts. The storm burst in September, 1959, when Miss Bennett announced in a letter to the Oldham Evening Chronicle that she had resigned as a trustee of the Oldham Repertory Theatre.

"For some time I had experienced anxiety about the way things were going at the theatre, and certain proposals being contemplated and supported by the full committee precipitated my resignation."

Two days later Mr. Harry Lomax, Director of Productions, revealed that the committee had decided not to renew his contract when it expired the following month.

All the members of the repertory company (except two who were on holiday) signed a letter to the Oldham Chronicle protesting at the committee's decision. A petition urging the reinstatement of Harry Lomax attracted about 700 signatures of club members. It all seemed like a replay of events ten years earlier. The committee defended its decision:

"For some considerable time there has been a persistent decrease in the income from box office receipts, and, while acknowledging the many contributory causes, it is imperative that we take any action which we feel would infuse new life and interest into the theatre. Without any reflection on the good work Mr. Lomax has undoubtedly rendered

in the past, we feel that the time has come when a change of director for one with a new approach, new ideas and a more extensive contact with artistes would benefit the theatre."

One factor which was always present in the events leading up to these periodical rows in the club was falling box office receipts. It was easy to blame the producer for not putting on the right kind of plays to attract bigger audiences but the real reasons for declining audiences went deeper than that. By 1959 television was eating more and more into the leisure time of all classes of the population. Car ownership and longer holidays – often spent abroad – were beginning to spread into sections of the working classes which had never enjoyed such things before. Football, the pub and the cinema were beginning to feel the adverse effects of this new affluence as their customers found other ways to spend their time and money. Those theatres which still existed, shared in the decline of custom.

While we are on this topic we might as well pursue it to the end. During the fifties and sixties the cinema put up a strong fight against television. Films in full colour became the norm and experiments were made in three-dimensional viewing. The latter was not a great success although the advent of the wide screen gave audiences an impression of 3D which created a little surge in cinema attendances. Several film spectaculars were produced and these helped to keep audiences from dwindling away, but the struggle ended when colour came to the TV screen at the start of the seventies. The cinema could no longer offer enough to compensate people for leaving the comfort of their own living room with the colour TV in the corner. During the sixties the Coliseum, as we shall see, managed to hold its own against its competitors. There was a feeling that TV, like a new toy, was perhaps losing its fascination and people were inclined to look outside the home once more for entertainment. However, the seventies brought not only colour TV and extra channels, but also new perils to menace the live theatre. A growing trade recession, industrial strife, galloping inflation and increasing unemployment led to increased costs and falling incomes. Theatre budgets failed to balance. Losses began to grow.

In the saloons of the Wild West, we are told, a notice was sometimes displayed:

"Don't shoot the pianist: he's doing his best."

When the economic going got rough in the post-war period some members of the Oldham Repertory Theatre Club were inclined to shoot the producer, others were eager to shoot the management committee. The tragedy was that the live theatre in the provinces was no longer able to survive without financial aid and eventually the club had to accept that unpalatable fact.

With this as the background let us return to the quarrel of 1959. The special meeting was held this time not because of a members' petition seeking a vote of no confidence in the committee, but it was called by the committee itself to see if it still retained the support of the club. Once again the meeting was long, noisy and packed with members. The committee got its vote of confidence – but only just. 183 supported the motion, 131 opposed and over 100 abstained.

The now vacant post of director of productions was advertised. Thirty-eight people applied for the job, and

Carl Paulsen, a talented and popular actor and a member of the Oldham Repertory Company, was appointed. He faced many problems. Expenditure exceeded income – the deficit was made up by fund-raising efforts; club membership was declining and had been losing 1,000 members a year throughout the fifties; and the proportion of theatre seats being filled for each performance was only in the 40% to 45% range. Weekly rep was imposing a severe strain on the company: standards were not as high as the club wished and play selection was beginning to prove difficult. A proposal had been made to overcome this problem earlier in the year. This involved acquiring the Hippodrome in Rochdale, forming two companies, and getting them to play alternate weeks at Oldham and Rochdale. This plan would allow each company to have two weeks of rehearsal for each play. The plan came to nothing because the Hippodrome, which had stood empty for a long time, would have required costly renovation to bring it up to regulation standards. (It was the implications of this proposed purchase which led to the resignation of Miss Bennett as a Coliseum trustee.)

Attendances improved a little during 1960, even though admission prices were increased. The committee's annual report made mention for the first time of the possibility of closure.

"What a catastrophe it would be to Oldham and the surrounding districts if we should ever have to close down through lack of support as so many other theatres have done," it said.

Somebody at the annual meeting suggested that the local authority might be asked to give financial support to the theatre. The suggestion was sternly rejected.

1961 found the theatre running hard but failing to move forward. Attendances were down by 7%, and there had been a sharp controversy in the local press about the content and quality of the play programme. Predictably there had been complaints about "swearing" in some of the plays. (We are now, of course, in the post-Chatterley era.) An attempt had been made to attract younger people by putting on monthly jazz concerts. Nevertheless, the balance sheet for the year showed a loss. It was clear that something more drastic than household economies were needed to stop the drift to insolvency.

Above **Judy Dickinson and Robert Keegan in "Murder at Quay Cottage", 1961.**

Left **Brian Seddon inspects the lighting equipment, 1960.**

Carl Paulsen as Charley's Aunt.

Kenneth Alan Taylor as "Mother Goose" with Jean Rimmer and Shirley Vaughan in 1963.

Barbara Mullaney (Knox) in 'Little Foxes', 1970.

The Coliseum goes public

The club took three important decisions which were implemented during the next two years. They involved:

1. The restructuring of the theatre staff.
2. An approach to Oldham Council and the Arts Council for financial aid.
3. Extensive renovation of the theatre to qualify for a public theatre licence.

In August, 1961, Derek Coleman, the theatre manager, was given notice. The posts of Manager and Director of Productions were combined into a new post of Theatre Administrator to which Carl Paulsen was appointed, with a Box Office Manageress and a Catering Manageress to assist him – and, in 1963, with Kenneth Alan Taylor as Assistant Producer. Fortunately Carl Paulsen was equal to the demands of the new job.

The basic renovation of the theatre was going to cost £20,000 and approaches were made to the local authority and to the Arts Council. Both bodies reacted favourably and promised £10,000 each with, as the chairman of the club, Frank Hanson, thankfully noted, "no strings attached". The club had evolved even more ambitious ideas and eventually came up with a £45,000 programme of reconstruction. Work began in August, 1964, and for 18 months plays continued to be produced under increasingly difficult conditions until on February 22, 1966, the renovated theatre was opened in style by Lord Rhodes.

Much of the old wooden structure of 1887 still remained up to the time of these alterations, but now all this had been removed. A new bar and coffee lounge had been built, a safety curtain installed and numerous other improvements carried out – including the removal of the old projection box.

There could be no doubt, that fine old lady, the Coliseum, had never looked better. Unfortunately the same could not be said for the gent she married in 1939, the Oldham Repertory Theatre Club. He was now middle-aged and was losing the sparkle and energy of youth. The effort of renovating the theatre took more out of him than anyone realised at the time and, in a world where a theatre had to run very hard indeed just to stay in the same place, he was beginning to lose the stamina to stay the course.

By August, 1968, the Coliseum was about the only theatre in the country doing weekly repertory and it was losing good actors and actresses who were no longer willing to rehearse a new play every week when they could work at other theatres on a fortnightly basis. In spite of all the fears that Oldham audiences would lose the habit of regular theatre-going, the inevitable step was taken. With "Suddenly Last Summer" (starring Pat Phoenix) the Coliseum changed over to fortnightly repertory. Unfortunately, while Oldham was debating and agonising over the change, other theatres had gone ahead and done it. Now many of them were turning to three-weekly repertory.

"I CAN'T WAIT TO READ THE CHRONICLE CRITIC TO SEE IF I ENJOYED IT!"

The club had always taken pride in standing on its own feet financially. Soaring costs and the seeming impossibility of raising audience figures regularly above 50% of capacity drove the club eventually – when it had no other choice – to ask first the Arts Council and later the local authority for an annual grant to help.

Yet the Coliseum was continuing to produce good, well-acted and well-produced plays. Some members of the club complained privately and publicly that the standard of play selection was too low. Others claimed as vociferously that there were too many "highbrow" plays which scared off the audiences. Yet another group were continually tut-tutting about too much sex and too many swear words in the plays presented. Which all seems to indicate that Carl Paulsen had the mixture just about right. An awful lot of club members had been asserting for years that the play reviews in the Oldham Evening Chronicle were "unfair" and put people off from going to the theatre. The facts do not support this complaint. If one looks through the reviews and comments for the last 35 years (as the author of this history has recently done), it is obvious that the local paper has consistently and fairly supported the theatre and its programmes. Admittedly it did at one time have a tendency to preach homilies about how grants of public money would lead to profligacy and waste on the part of the theatre management, but that was an amiable weakness to which all editors are particularly prone. The Oldham Evening Chronicle has been a good friend to the Coliseum.

It was obvious to most people that by the beginning of the seventies the Coliseum was running into serious trouble. Costs continued to rise steeply, equipment was wearing out, the theatre roof needed to be replaced and the balance sheets were showing a regular, growing loss. On Thursday, May 10, 1973, Carl Paulsen died suddenly at the age of 47. During his 13 years at the Coliseum, Carl had, more than anyone else, stamped his personality upon the theatre. Some months earlier his photograph had appeared in the Evening Chronicle and beneath it were these words which might well serve as his epitaph:

"Carl Paulsen, Rep administrator, manager, producer, director, actor, and the man who locks up when everybody else has gone home."

Pat Phoenix in rehearsal with
Carl Paulsen.

Time of peril

Construction of a new stage tower, fly gallery and workshop in 1973.

The next five years were sad ones for the Coliseum. The Theatre Club was terminally ill; its day was past and repertory theatres could no longer be owned and sustained by private clubs. The times were against it. Strikes, the oil crisis, inflation, unemployment, the three-day week, and other afflictions did nothing to encourage people to acquire the habit of going to the theatre. In any case, they all had colour TV at home. Audiences at the Coliseum dwindled, costs soared and income fell.

Producers came and went – the usual sign that things were not going right. Victor Graham and Patrick Masefield each lasted less than a year, John Jardine, as Director of Productions made it into his second year, as did Brian Howard as Artistic Director. They all pumped hard, but the water kept coming in and the ship continued to sink lower in the sea of economic troubles. Salvage tugs were needed to tow the ship to a harbour where she could be refitted and launched again with a new crew.

The £50,000 reconstruction of the stage area nearing completion in 1974. Oldham Corporation and the Arts Council contributed £20,000 each towards the cost.

Unfortunately the obvious salvage tugs – the local authorities – were otherwise engaged in coping with local government reorganisation and were too busy to attend to sinking theatres. However, by 1976 the newly created Greater Manchester Council was aiding the Coliseum with a grant and Oldham Metropolitan Borough increased its own grant. Both bodies insisted on increased representation on the management committee. The Arts Council continued its support. Nevertheless, the losses accumulated.

These four years of crisis brought out the worst in many members of the Oldham Repertory Theatre Club. The annual meeting in June, 1974, was yet another of the noisy, crowded meetings that had characterised earlier periods of crisis. There were letters to the press, angry accusations and endless gossip. By 1977 it was evident that the end was not far off. The club could no longer meet its commitments and could no longer maintain the theatre. If Oldham was going to keep the Coliseum as a live theatre, then the only course open was for the Oldham Metropolitan District to take the building off the hands of the club, arrange for it to be run by a new board of management and give it a new start. To acquire and repair the theatre would cost about £46,000; to continue to run it as a theatre would involve the grant-aiding bodies in a regular expenditure of tens of thousands of pounds. Was there any reason why the town – not the wealthiest of local authorities – should shoulder this burden?

Fortunately the attitudes of public bodies at this time were changing. The post-war rush to build houses had resulted in the construction of new towns and housing estates which often consisted of nothing more than houses and shops. The resulting social problems made it clear that something more was needed to create stable and healthy communities. So, too, the decline of the old manufacturing industries left economic holes in many of Britain's towns which they tried hard to fill by seeking to attract new businesses to set up in place of the old ones. To do this, it began to be realised, the town itself had to be made attractive to the managers and executive staff of the businesses looking for a new place to settle. Obviously a town where leisure provisions had died out with the former industries was going to rank low in attractiveness. So local authorities began to preserve what theatres and concert halls and other facilities they still possessed, and to build new swimming pools, sports halls and other entertainment centres. In the light of these new ideas it was seen that Oldham could not really afford to lose the Coliseum. Not only would the town lose an attractive amenity, but the closure would be bad publicity for the town and, indeed, for the wider region of Greater Manchester.

Oldham, therefore, agreed to buy and to maintain the theatre and, together with the Greater Manchester Council and the Arts Council, it set out to give regular financial aid to keep the theatre going. Once more the Coliseum had been rescued. Her former protector who had kept her for nearly 40 years had to be deserted. She had become an expensive lady to keep and needed wealthier patrons than the Oldham Repertory Theatre Club.

The Club passed away without anybody taking much notice of the event. In any case, the prophets of doom were busy foretelling the inevitable demise of the Coliseum as well. Readers of this centenary history might well pause at this point and mentally salute those thousands of Oldham people who, through this club, saved and made famous the Oldham Coliseum.

"THEY'RE YELLING 'AUTHOR!' GET OUT THERE AND CONFESS!"

Ian Masters, John Jardine and Karen Petrie in "Mother Goose", 1973.

Husband and wife team, Kenneth Alan Taylor and Judith Barker in "Rattle of a Simple Man", 1964.

Under new management

Although Oldham had taken over the theatre and was prepared to keep it running it was on the clear understanding that the newly-appointed management board must keep within its budget for the future. For its part the new board was acutely aware that the key to this particular problem was to be found in satisfactory appointments to the posts of Administrator and Artistic Director. The board could not afford to make a wrong choice: there were to be no second chances and if the theatre continued to fail it would, within two years, be closed for good.

We are now dealing with events only eight years ago and it is not easy to see them in proper historical perspective, but I doubt if the historian of the Coliseum's second hundred years will dissent from the opinion that the management committee made the right start in 1978 by appointing Kenneth Alan Taylor as Artistic Director and Chris Moxon as Administrator. In the former they had a fine actor and director associated with the Coliseum over many years and who knew Oldham audiences, and in the latter they found a competent and astute administrator. By happy chance the man who became

Chairman of the Board, Councillor Ray Whitehead, found himself in his element in that role and formed an essential and successful link between the theatre staff and the board. This trio launched the theatre on its new voyage and steered it through the rough waters of the eighties.

Kenneth Alan Taylor, having set the new Coliseum off on its new course with a series of very successful productions, resigned in 1982 to everyone's regret. Caroline Smith filled in as Artistic Director for a few months and then Pat Trueman occupied the post from 1982 to 1985. The present director, John Retallack, is finding that the eighties are proving as challenging and as unpredictable as previous decades. Audiences increase and diminish according to no known law. The Arts Council, the Greater Manchester Council and Oldham Metropolitan Borough Council have given their powerful support to the theatre. Recently the abolition of the Greater Manchester Council has made it necessary for the money from that particular source to be provided from elsewhere. Money is always the problem.

This centenary celebration includes an appeal to set up an Endowment Fund of sufficient size to provide a buffer against future shocks and blows. The Coliseum deserves to be supported.

John Retallack, Artistic Director, 1985– .

A forward planning meeting. Chris Moxon (Administrator), Councillor Anthony Goldstone M.B.E. (Greater Manchester Council), Pat Trueman (Artistic Director) and Ray Whitehead (Chairman of the Board).

The auditorium, 1986.

The revamped theatre bar in 1985.

Chris Bond at the lighting board, 1986.

It's the play that matters

The Coliseum, like any other theatre, is only a box, a container for what is the real business of the theatre: the production of a play and the interaction between actors and audience. The history of the Coliseum cannot be written without some account of the plays and players of the past century. Unfortunately the performing arts are the most ephemeral – unless recorded on film or tape. Once the curtain falls the performance of a play continues to live only in the memories of the audience, and as memories fade and people die or forget, so the

performance slips into oblivion. How can we write about the performances of the past hundred years? Standards change and memory often improves on fact. Would Sarah Bernhardt, Henry Irving or Ellen Terry be given top rank as actors today? The acting styles of the last century would probably give modern audiences a fit of the giggles.

Fortunately we are not required to make these impossible comparisons and it is enough to record that certain past performances were able to enchant people to such an extent that the memory stays with them for the rest of their lives. What a magical evening it must have been for one little girl nearly 60 years ago:

"I am writing to you of a memory of mine as a child of perhaps five or six years old which was some 58 or 59 years ago. I was taken to see the Christmas panto 'Cinderella'. I remember sitting upstairs, probably in 'the gods'.

My mother read in the paper that Cinderella's ball gown was trimmed with diamonds and crystals and had cost £100, which was a fortune then to us. Of course I had to wait until the very last scene to see this dress – that is all I remember of the show: the last scene.

In my young eyes it was the most beautiful dress and shoes that sparkled and glittered. I will always remember it. I wonder who played the part of Cinders?" (Mrs. Edith Druggitt of Scouthead)

Two or three years earlier a young Oldham boy also acquired a lifelong memory when his father took him to the Coliseum to see a variety show round about 1925, but, unlike Edith, he was not struck by beauty:

"Amongst the artists was Samson, the World's Strongest Man. His feats included bending steel bars and breaking steel chains after they had been inspected by the audience. He also lifted heavy weights by his teeth. Whilst lying on his back a small swing roundabout was placed on his chest and operated with four adults sat in the seats, and afterwards he finished his act by lying face downwards on the stage and a small car passed over his body." (Mr. A. Hallett of Lees)

The Coliseum has staged nearly 2,000 productions since the Repertory Theatre Club took it over in 1939. Most of these were very ordinary plays, enjoyable enough but not mentally demanding. Nevertheless the Coliseum has always taken pride in presenting a fair proportion of classical and modern plays of intellectual value. Sometimes such plays attracted good audiences, but often they did not. When, in 1954, the BBC televised a play at the Coliseum, acted by the repertory company, it had to be Dodie Smith's lightweight romance, "I Capture the Castle". Locally the TV reception was bad – trouble at the transmitter – but the choice of play and the way the BBC handled the broadcast were disastrous. The audience figure for that week reached 61% which was good for that particular period when theatres were suffering the first impact of the competition from television.

The fifties, of course, saw the Archers set off on their phenomenal radio career. In 1953 the script-writers, Edward Mason and Geoffrey Webb, decided to cash in on their radio success and turned out a play based on Ambridge and the well-known characters of the serial. The Oldham Rep took it on and became the first repertory company to stage it. "A mild and rambling piece," said a critic, "produced in a mild and unexceptional manner. There was no particular urgency about the acting, but not even brilliant acting could do much with the material". However, Oldham audiences obviously loved it and flocked to see it. An audience figure of 90% capacity was achieved.

Mike Harding's "One Night Stand", 1981.

For the centenary of the birth of George Bernard Shaw, Harry Lomax put on that author's play, "Misalliance". It was well produced and brought good reviews but attracted audiences of only 49% capacity. Herman Wouk's "The Caine Mutiny Court Martial", staged with an all male cast of 16, managed only 45% capacity audiences. There did not lack people to claim that Oldham audiences responded only to second-rate plays, but, in all fairness, it is difficult to prove that Oldham audiences were any worse than those in other towns. In any case, a nation that can support "The Mousetrap" in an unbroken run of 33 years can hardly lay claim to high standards of taste in drama.

The year 1957 saw the Coliseum producing five premieres and, in addition, staging the current controversial play, "Look Back in Anger" by John Osborne – ("Please note that junior members will not be admitted to this play") – which brought in 57% capacity audiences. The previous year Thora Hird had packed them in playing Ada Thorp in Walter Greenwood's "Saturday Night at the Crown", (86%). Even John Galsworthy's "Windows" got 57% audiences.

In those days the break-even point for a play of average costs was 60% of audience capacity; below that the theatre was running at a loss. So one's sympathy must go out to the play selectors of the last 50 years. Their scope for putting on challenging plays was very limited and they certainly could never afford to gain the reputation of presenting "boring" and "difficult" plays. To keep audiences above the 60% level, especially after 1968 when weekly rep was changed to fortnightly, required a rare mixture of skill and luck from selectors, producers and actors. In the seventies the luck began to run out. In 1953, for example, the audiences ranged as follows:

Out of 48 plays produced, 12 attracted audiences of over 70% capacity, 32 had between 50% and 70%, and only four fell into the 40% to 49% group.

During the seventies the number of plays produced was halved because of the change from weekly to fortnightly rep. Unfortunately the audiences decreased too. The figures slipped down the scale and during the last few years of the Oldham Repertory Theatre Club, audiences of well below 50% capacity were the norm. Yet it is hard to say that the type and quality of the plays were any worse.

The new Coliseum, with Kenneth Alan Taylor as Artistic Director and Chris Moxon as Administrator, managed, to everyone's relief, to attract audiences, but the early eighties produced yet another dip in audience figures. It is all very unpredictable and there is no doubt that the Coliseum in its second hundred years will have to endure these periodical desertions by its audiences, but so long as the play selection is sound and the standards of production and acting are maintained, this history shows that the audiences will support the Coliseum. The theatre belongs to Oldham and the town has every reason to be proud of the splendid centenarian.

Judith Barker and Malcolm Scates in "Me Mam Sez", 1986.